ACKNOWLEDGEMENTS

The Chairman and members of the Shere, Gomshall and Peaslake Local History Society are grateful to an earlier generation of local historians who did the initial work on this booklet. They were Sir Jack Sutherland-Harris, K.C.V.O.,C.B., Mr. Kenneth Gravett, M.Sc. (Eng.), F.S.A., Mr. R.L. Swan, B.Sc., D.I.C., Mrs. Sylvia Bright and Mrs. Jeanne Goldsmith.

The original notes on the history of the houses of Shere and Gomshall together with maps, first appeared in *Surrey History* Nos. 1 & 2 issued by the Surrey Local History Council (now the Local History Committee of the Surrey Archaeological Society).

New information has been provided by Dennis Turner, the late Peter Gray, other members of the Domestic Buildings Research Group and local residents. Thanks to the Karlsson family for the digital design, layout and photographs in 2003.

Other Titles Published by the
Shere, Gomshall & Peaslake Local History Society

Shere, Gomshall & Peaslake: a Short History
The Tillingbourne Story
A Tannery in Gomshall
Shere: A Surrey Village in Maps *(published by Surrey Archaeological Society)*

G000256054

First Published 1976
Reprinted 1977
ɔvised & Reprinted 1981
Reprinted 1985
Reprinted 1992
Reprinted 1993
Revised & Reprinted 1995
Reprinted 1997
Revised & Reprinted 2003
Reprinted 2005
Reprinted 2008

INTRODUCING THE OLD HOUSES OF SHERE PARISH

Shere and Gomshall are both mentioned in the Domesday Survey in 1086 as Essira and Gumsele (Guma's shelf). The Poll Tax return of 1380 records 166 persons over the age of fifteen in the vill of Shere, which then included Cranleigh and 267 in the vill of Gomshall which included Peaslake and Ewhurst. During the fifteenth, sixteenth and seventeenth centuries the population grew and concentrated in the centres of Shere, Gomshall and Peaslake with houses of weavers, tailors and craftsmen such as blacksmiths and wheelwrights, some of whom were also yeomen and husbandmen. Much new building and rebuilding went on from about 1580 to 1640, based on prosperity from sheep and wool. While outwardly Shere houses are a mixture of styles from the fifteenth to the twentieth centuries, the central portion of the village is still fundamentally 16th and 17th century, with many timber framed houses of which several were originally built on the 'open hall' pattern.

There are fewer old houses in Gomshall than Shere, but they tend to be larger and more important. The majority of the smaller Peaslake houses are concentrated in the valley with the larger ones scattered in the farming country towards the Hurtwood. Shere and Gomshall (with Peaslake) each had two manors; Shere Eborum and Shere Vachery, Gomshall Netley and Gomshall Tower Hill. Both villages had watermills on the Tillingbourne, the tanneries were concentrated in Gomshall. Shere, Gomshall and Peaslake now constitute one parish. We are lucky to have a surviving record of the 1380 Poll Tax for the vills of Shere (with Cranleigh) and Gomshall (with Ewhurst). It is interesting to find that 50 of the 433 personal names from 1380 are recognisable as past and present property names in the four villages.

The following notes on the old houses are based on the examination of the house structures and on study of documentary sources including estate plans, the Tithe Map, manorial records and deeds at the Surrey History Centre.

This booklet is divided into three sections: Gomshall, Peaslake and Shere. Each section has notes on the houses to be found in that village, and a map to show their location.

Gomshall map - page 8/9
Peaslake map - page 16/17
Shere map - inside back cover.

More details of the history of the villages can be found in the other titles published by the Society, listed on the preceding page.

OLD GOMSHALL HOUSES

(1) Towerhill Manor, was the principal house in the manor of Gomshall Towerhill or

East Gomshall. It is described in 1568 as 'a house within a mote' consisting of a hall, two cellars, one kitchen and other chambers. Much of this open hall house, dating from the early sixteenth century, still exists at the back of the main manor house. It was built either for the first Sir Edward Bray, or for Sir Edmund Walsingham from whom he bought the manor. The main house was built as a new wing about 1600-10, probably by the third Edward Bray, after his marriage in 1603. This new wing has Jacobean panelling and fireplaces, a newel staircase and an unusual embossed heraldic ceiling decoration. About 1680 the parlour of the old house was pulled down and a new corner and staircase built with Bargate stone walls and brick dressings, probably by the fifth Edward Bray. The five-bay south façade to the Jacobean wing was a rebuild by the sixth Edward Bray before 1739. The house was occupied by the Bray family until the death of the Rev. George Bray in 1803. It was restored by a tenant, Mr Tatham, in 1908.

(2) Malthouse Cottages, formerly Skinners in Gomshall Netley, is a good quality

house, with notable chimneys. Originally a three-bay medieval house with a fine two-bay parlour wing to the south, with ornate timber work on the front and fine chamfer moulding and stops in the main ground floor girders. It was probably built for John Gatton who died in 1616. This wing has a through-purlin roof supported by flat curved angle-struts, but no collars. The crosswing at the north end was refronted in Bargate stone about the end of the seventeenth century when it belonged to Thomas Coe. The first reference to a malthouse, which may have been part of the house or attached to it, is in 1677 and the property is still described as 'a house with a malthouse' in 1843. It belonged to Thomas Coe and his daughter's Mower descendants from 1678 to 1828 when it became part of the Netley estate.

(3) Goose Green Cottage, has a back part dating from about 1650 and a front part

from about 1750, but it is not identifiable in the records.

(4) Gomshall Mill, may be on the site of a mill at Gumsele mentioned in the Domesday  Survey of 1086, but there is no evidence. It was an important part of the demesne lands of Gomshall Towerhill and is shown in a1568 inventory as 'a watermill worth 66s.8d a year beyond the cost of repairs' and so one of the manor's most valuable possessions. The first record of the lease of a mill is in 1611 when the third Edward Bray leased it to John Chennell for £16 a year; it then consisted of 'a watermill and millhouse containing a cornmill and maltmill under one roof and a millpond'. The present five-bay timber- framed mill building is probably early 17th century and the two-bay miller's house with chimney and bacon loft at the north end is early to mid 17th century. At the end of the 17th century, when let to Woods, it was said to contain four cornmills. In 1750 it was sold by the Brays to the tenant, David Harris of Shere; he sold to Thomas Withall, miller of Fetcham, in 1786. It was sold again in 1822, probably to William Southon, who also owned the baker's shop (Vaughans) in Shere. In 1839 the undershot mill was re-designed as an overshot mill with a cast iron mill wheel instead of a wooden one. After William Southon's death in 1850, the mill was bought by Kelseys, along with the baker's, and later they built the neighbouring house, 'Bourneside', now 'The Gallery'. In 1897 George Egerton bought it, and his nephews became the tenants, which they remained after he sold to Sir Reginald Bray in 1902 - a resumption of Bray ownership after 250 years, which lasted to 1950. A little later it ceased to be a mill and is now a restaurant. The pillory is a recent addition.

(5) The Black Horse, is the remaining part of a property which seems to have begun  as a malthouse built about 1690, rented from Gomshall Towerhill for a grain of pepper, and then belonging to William Amey. It later became a brewery which remained until 1930. The inn appears to have been built in the 19th century and the name The Black Horse appears in the 1823 rent roll. It belonged to the Reffells for well over a hundred years from 1812.

(6) Edmonds and Churchfield Farm, seem to have been a small subsidiary manor in  Gomshall Netley, owned by Nicholas Shenfield in the 15th century. He probably built the earliest part of the house, which dates from about 1450 and consisted of a two-bay open hall, a two storey parlour at the west end with crown post roof and a two storey service wing to the east of the hall. In the early 16th century it belonged to the Redfords and later in that century to Thomas Elyot. He was a citizen and draper of London and probably put in the central fireplace in the eastern bay of the hall between 1580 and 1600 and added another bay at the service end. The original chimney is still there. His heirs were his two daughters and from about 1650 to 1860 the property was held in two undivided halves. One of these was acquired by the Evelyns of Wotton about 1608 and the other, somewhat later, by the Husseys of Sutton Place, Abinger. This part then went with the Sutton and Netley estates until in 1860 John Fraser of Netley also acquired the Evelyn half. From the mid-18th to the mid-19th centuries, members of the Burchett family were the tenants of Edmonds and its 150 acre farm. During this time a number of alterations were made, probably about 1830, giving the house its present form, including the stuccoed exterior and the monkey puzzle tree.

(7) Craddocks, was originally a 15th century open hall house. The two-bay open hall

remains, raised in height when it was floored over in the 17th century. A mid- to late 15th century crosswing remains in the centre of the present house, with a 17th century parlour added to the west. The brick fronting is early 18th century. Henry Levett owned in 1556 when he sold to the Astone family who held for 100 years and may have rebuilt the original hall. Later two branches of the Frost family owned, from 1745 to 1860.

(8) Netley House, was originally a red brick house, comprising the central portion of

the present house, built about 1790 by Edward Shallett Lomax on the demesne lands of Gomshall Netley manor. These lands had been sold in 1642 by the fourth Edward Bray, to his brother-in-law, William Heath, from Sussex and had later become part of the Sutton Place, Abinger and Netley estate. Lomax built it for his own occupation and moved there from Sutton Place, Abinger, which was then pulled down. Netley House was burnt down in the middle of the 19th century, and rebuilt about 1860 when the two-storey wings were added on each side. Commandeered by the Army in 1940, it was bought by the National Trust in 1942 and is currently the office of an architectural practice. It is not open to the public.

(9) Netley Farm, is a house built within the last 100 years in place of an earlier Netley

House, a farmhouse which had been part of the Gomshall Netley demesne lands belonging to the Brays in the 16th century but sold in 1642.

(10) King John House, formerly Tannery or Old Tannery House and later Ivy House, in

the manor of Gomshall Towerhill was shown on a 1788 estate plan. It then belonged to Rev. George Bray as a mansion house and a tanyard with a considerable number of buildings. The main part of the present house is in fine Jacobean brick, built about 1620 by the Bignolds, who were tanners and appear to have come here about 1550 from Cobham. There are the remains of an earlier timber-framed house at the back, with substantial beams downstairs and a crown post roof dating from about 1500 or earlier. In its layout the Jacobean house closely resembles the slightly earlier Jacobean part of Towerhill Manor. It looks as if the Bignolds built it in emulation of the Brays. It remained in the Bignold family until bought by the Rev. George Bray in 1787, having descended to a daughter, Mrs Anne Brayne, in 1700 and then to her daughters. Two of them emigrated to Virginia, USA where they married and their descendants sold in 1787. The tanyard seems to have remained in use until about the end of the 18th century, latterly on lease to the Eastmans, who had another tanyard in Queen Street. There is an old tradition that the house was built shortly after the great plague of 1665 from profits on hides collected free in London, but neither the structure nor the documents support this and in fact the house appears to have been built a good deal earlier.

(11) Gomshall Tannery Site and Nos. 2—9 Station Road, were formerly two old

houses on the north side of the Tillingbourne called Jordells and Yardleys, with a tanyard on the south side across the Packhorse Bridge. One, a four-bay timber-framed house with a crown post roof built in the second quarter of the 16th century remains and has now been adapted for community use as Tanyard Hall. The other early house seems to have been removed towards the end of the 19th century. The property belonged to the Goddards for most of the 17th century and then to the Coes from 1688-1815. From 1815 until 1835 William Johnson was master tanner and at his death in 1835 it passed to John Evershed of Albury, his son-in-law. The Eversheds built the substantial Victorian house and out buildings, parts of which have now become the row of houses, Nos 2-9 Station road. The Tannery was owned by the Gilligans of Reading after the Eversheds. A large part of it was burnt down in 1892 but rebuilt the same year. It was bought by the Vesteys in 1922 and after temporary closure during the depression continued in Vestey ownership as a successful enterprise and major local employer until 1987 when it was sold and closed down the following year. The Tannery site has now been developed for housing. [For further information see booklet *A Tannery in Gomshall*]

(12) Grovers Cottages, were originally one house built in 1826 by William King, miller

of Netley Mill and extended by his daughter, Kesia Stedman and her husband, Richard.

(13) The Compasses, was also built by the Stedmans in 1830, but soon sold to John

Sherman of Shere. It was originally a beer shop. It seems to have become an inn in 1886, when it was leased to a Guildford brewery company.

(14) 9—12 Queen Street, was formerly a farm house called Loves with a manor record going back to 1557 when it was John Levett's. The oldest part, now at the back, was an open hall house of the 15th century, and faced east towards the old track running parallel with the present Queen Street. A large timber-framed addition to the west towards Queen Street was built about 1550. Before 1581 it passed to the Gatton family who owned for nearly 200 years until 1758, when it was bought by George Eastmund or Eastman. Belonging to it in the 18th century was a third Gomshall Tannery operated by the Eastmans, but this was broken up in 1794. It lay to the north of the house, near the marsh.

(15) Gomshall Lodge, seems to have been built by John King, a builder, before 1823.

It appears on a rent roll on land called Donningsfield, part of Loves, which he had bought in 1815.

(16) Monks House, was formerly Gravel Pits farmhouse. It was built on the waste of

the manor of Gomshall Netley in 1663 by Thomas Street. He appears to have been a blacksmith and the house he built was of very high quality. The main block was built round a central chimney with a two-bay crosswing at the east end on which the original infilling of flint and brick can be seen. It has a queen strut and through-purlin roof with no windbraces. From 1724-1857 the farm belonged to the Frost family. The 19th century additions at the back were made by the Frasers of Netley.

(17) Colekitchen Farm, is an early 17th century two-bay, timber-framed, end-chimney house, with a late 17th century two storey wing with attics. Thomas Redford was a tenant in 1708, when he was allocated a seat in the church. An agreement between him and Edward Bray in 1707 mentions 'house, barns, stables etc. sometime since erected'.

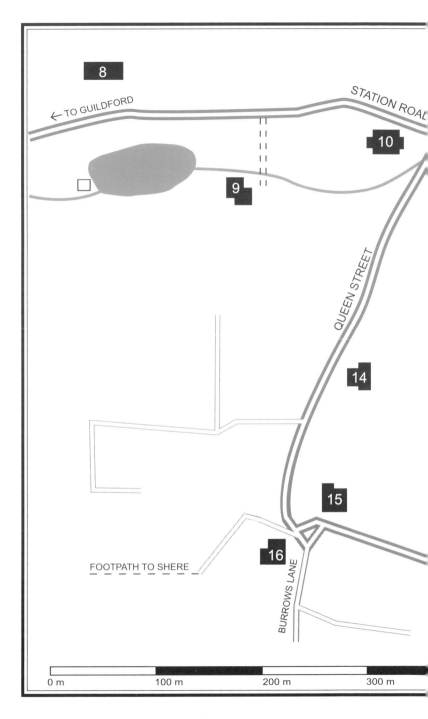

8
← TO GUILDFORD
STATION ROAD
10
9
QUEEN STREET
14
15
16
BURROWS LANE
FOOTPATH TO SHERE

| 0 m | 100 m | 200 m | 300 m |

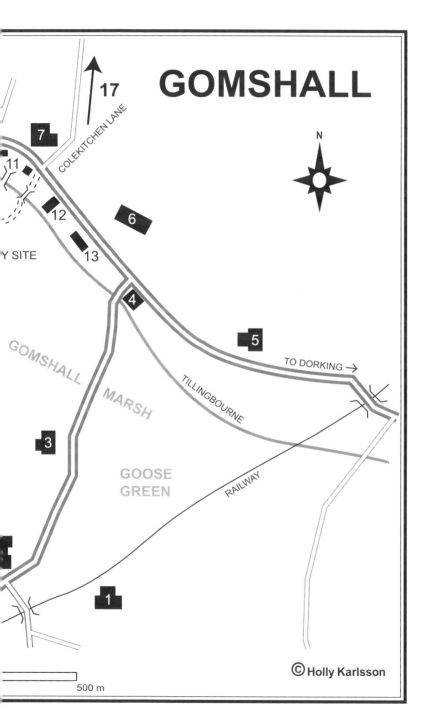

GOMSHALL

N

17

COLEKITCHEN LANE

7

11

12

6

Y SITE

13

4

5

TO DORKING →

GOMSHALL

MARSH

TILLINGBOURNE

3

GOOSE
GREEN

RAILWAY

1

© Holly Karlsson

500 m

OLD PEASLAKE HOUSES

(1) Quakers Orchard, formerly Botchery Butchers and then Burying Place Farm, has a brick front block, with butt-side purlin roof of about 1750, with some re-used timbers from an earlier house. An older, smaller block, to the south-west, built of stone with brick dressings and anglestrut roof, may have been built as a Quaker meeting place in the second half of the 17th century, adjoining the earlier house. About 1850, dormers in the main block were rebuilt, the parapet added or rebuilt and a new staircase installed. Two additional wings to the south-west were built about 1910 and 1930. In 1367 the land belonged to William Botchery. In 1532 it was John Seman's and the earlier house, first recorded in 1624, was probably built by the Semans, who included the prominent Quaker, Thomas Seman (owner 1644-1700). He probably built the meeting house and established the burying place in the grounds. The mid-18th century house would have been built by the Woods (1746-1834) and was inherited by their relatives, the Goldhawks of Hazel Hall. As part of the latter estate, it was owned by the Cubitts from 1864-1919. The 1930's addition was by Sir Adrian Boult.

(2) Hazel Hall, formerly Hazelholt, consisting of the large, brick, Georgian-type block at the eastern end with small servants' wing behind, was built to replace an earlier house, but on a new site The original large chimneys have been removed. The stone-walled north wing in polygonal rubble with garnetting, was built as a stable in the early 19th century and converted later in that century when other additions were also made. A Thomas of Hazelholt is recorded as owning before 1532. There was a house belonging to the Champions in 1619, but no parts remain. They were followed by the Slarkes (1630-51). The present house may have been built by the Snellings (1651-1718) and altered by John Hide (1759-63) or Benjamin Berwick (1766-78). He left it to his daughter Mary, second wife of William Sherlock of Cottells, Shere and he retained it until his death in 1794. From 1799-1870, the Goldhawks owned, and then the Cubitts (1870-1919), with FEJ Blackburne as occupier for many years.

(3) Burchett's Hollow, formerly Clarks, is a timber-framed house of which the older section, with large square panels and no jowls to the posts, is mid 17th century. It has two bays, but has lost another bay and its original chimney. The roof has through side-purlins and angle-struts. Later in the 17th century, another section was added to the south-east, having a roof with collars and three struts and some lighter timber framing on the back wall. This has a large brick chimney with an oven and spit rack. Some encasing in stone with garnetting was done possibly in the early 18th century. Built perhaps by the Husseys of Sutton, who owned in the second half of the 17th century but sold to John Amey in 1704. John Woods of Burying Place owned in mid 18th century and later the Goldhawks of Hazel Hall.

(4) **Purser's Farm,** named after Adam Purs, who held in 1367, belonged to the  Redfords from before 1532 to 1627 when it was sold to Samuel Symonds, a citizen of London. It was given to the parish of St Saviour's, Southwark, for the use of the poor of the parish, and was so held until the 20th century. The house was described as a capital one in 1637, so it was probably an important farmhouse in Hoe then; but the present brick farmhouse dates from the late 17th century to the late 18th century.

(5) **Old Rock Cottage,** formerly part of either Stonesland or Pursers, it is a late 16th  century timber-framed house, originally with two rooms on the ground floor and a chimney added at the north end beyond the smoke bay. The roof is a queen-strut, side-purlin. The front was replaced in stone at the end of the 17th century or early 18th. The only manor record is in the late 18th century rent book describing it as 'John Chennell's house that pays a red rose in rent to the manor'.

(6) **Old Well Cottage,** was part of Stonesland and contains the oldest remaining  structural work in Peaslake. Originally a four-bay open hall house (one bay now lost), it was built at the end of the 14th century, with a crown post roof. Weathering of timbers suggests the house may have been derelict for 100 years, until taken in hand about 1700 when a chimney was inserted. Manor records start in 1722, so Edward Hooker, who owned then, may have restored it. Hookers owned until they sold to Edmund Lomax of Netley in 1798.

(7) **Hoe Farm,** formerly Francis Tenement, was a mid to late 15th century open hall  house; one-and-a-half timber-framed bays remain in the north-west section. It has a large central tie beam, heavy braces and short, plain crown post, but a half-bay to the west is missing. The two-bay crosswing to the east, with a crown post in its front gable, is probably the first house, to which the north-west wing was added. Chimney inserted about 1600 and substantial addition with queen strut roof built to the south in early to mid 17th century. The land was William Francis' in 1367, and the Francis family, prominent in Shere records in the 16th century may have built the original house. In 1619 it belonged to Francis Allen, who sold to John Amey, and his descendants remained owners to 1746. It became part of Netley estate in 1797.

(8) Keepers, formerly Burges Hoe, is a timber framed house of about 1580-1620 with

three bays and a roof with tall, thin queen struts. There may have been an additional parlour bay to the north, now missing. The hall kitchen has a rare mark of the old settle. A new high quality brick and stone front was built about 1720. George Tickner may have built the house as he sold it in 1622 to John Hillier. For most of the 17th century it belonged to the Morgan Sherlocks. In 1718 William Stovold acquired it and his family owned to 1781 when it became part of the Netley estate.

(9) Oak Hill Cottage, formerly Ludsly Pursers, is a timber-framed house of about

1550 with three bays representing parlour and hall kitchen. There was probably a service bay at the south-east end, now lost. It has a roof with collar, side purlins and queen struts. An original smoke bay was replaced by a chimney about a generation after first building. The stone front is late 17th or early 18th century. Goddards owned from before 1620 to about 1720 and probably built the original house. In 1777 it became part of the Netley estate. Further alterations were carried out about 1850 when it was converted into two cottages.

(10) Old Rydings, formerly Woodcrofts, a part of Francis Tenement but also called

Basinghouse, is an early 17th century timber-framed house. It consists of a main block and a large crosswing added a generation or two later. Roof has queen struts and collars, but main posts have no jowls. An ancient yew stands beside the house. Manor records call it 'a house lately built' in 1619 when sold with 20 acres to Edward Lee by Francis Allen, owner of Francis Tenement (now Hoe Farm). He may have built it as a speculation. In the late 17th century it became the property of the Husseys of Sutton then of the Ameys, followed by William Stovold and his heirs, until it became part of the Netley estate in 1797.

(11) Hollybush Cottage, formerly a part of Larks called Redacre, is a timber-framed

house of the mid 17th century, re-fronted in stone perhaps in the 18th century. The roof is queen strut with side purlins. The oldest part is of two-bays around a narrow bay containing the chimney. Another bay was added to the west, perhaps within 50 years. Manor records start in 1644, perhaps the time that the house was built when Thomas Pearding sells four acres to John Stonehill. In 1713 Thomas Frost bought and it remained Frost property until 1802 when it became part of Netley estate.

(12) Well and Rydings Cottages, formerly Scuddiers, are timber-framed and built at

the end of the 17th century. The roof has angle struts and through side purlins, no collars or wind braces. Timbers are light and much replaced. A house was first mentioned in 1698 when Morgan Sherlock junior died and left to Robert Sherlock. In 1717 William Stovold bought it and his family owned to 1761 when it became part of Netley estate.

(13) Southcots, was part of Woodcrofts (No.10). The records say that two cottages

were built here in 1829 by Benjamin Edser. The roof has a ridge piece and light rafters and the stone walls with rat-trap bond brickwork belong to this period but the chimney seems to belong to an earlier house of around 1700. A large addition is dated 1892.

(14) Mackies Hill, is an early to late 17th century timber-framed house which had one

room on each floor and a chimney with oven and bacon loft, an added bay and queen strut roof. There is a large extension at the back made in the 20th century, using an 18th century Sussex barn. No separate manor record but apparently a cottage on Spurfold.

(15) Pippins, appears to be another cottage on Spurfold; the old part is of stone with

light timber-framing at north-east end; it was built about 1700 or a little later.

(16) Lindeth Cottage, is two storied with a gabled roof, built on Upper Spurfold about

1650 in random rubble with garnetting and a string course in English bond. The main block has three bays with a large chimney at south end. The roof has queen struts, collars and side purlins. The large wing to the west is part of the original house. A brick porch was added before 1700. Built by Robert Snelling and his wife Elizabeth, who owned Spurfold with her father William Gosden, but they soon sold to the Husseys of Sutton Place. Thomas Frost bought in 1714 and his family owned to 1798 when it became part of Netley estate.

(17) Sawyers, was part of Spurfold and belonged in 1723 to George Snelling along

with a parcel of manor waste enclosed for a shop. These descended to James Dibble. References to the house call it Pislake and in 1761 say it bore the sign of Admiral Vernon's head; it appears to have been the Peaslake alehouse in the 18th century. The structure has been much altered, the road level has been raised considerably and a part that stood further back has gone. The original stone house, with no garnetting, was built in the late 17th or early 18th century, possibly by George Snelling. Largely rebuilt above the old floor level at the beginning of the 20th century. A blacksmith's shop is shown just to the south on the Tithe Map of 1843.

(18) Western Cottages, were formerly the Workhouse, built as such in the 1720s,  replacing an earlier cottage. Main block, of two storeys and attics, has five bays and a central chimney; a two-bay section of similar construction and date is at the back and is said to have contained a mortuary. The attics were probably dormitories. The roof has tie beams, collars and through side-purlins, but is of very light construction. In the centre of the back is a bakehouse built between 1780 and 1850. The manor record starts with a cottage in 1675, built on manor waste or common. The New Poor House is mentioned in the church visitation report of 1724. By 1733 it is being held in trust for the poor by John Harding, and was the Shere Parish Workhouse for 100 years. Other Trustees were John Holland, 1737, Richard Pinches, 1759 and Thomas Frost of Gravel Pits 1800. It was sold in 1839 to Rowland Goldhawk of Hazel Hall and later with his estate to the Cubitt trustees.

(19) East View, formerly the main part of Bowbrook's Cottages, is a three-bay timber-  framed house, built originally as one house with a chimney at the south end early in the 17th century. The roof has side-purlins not in line and angle struts without collars. A chimney was added at the north end when it was made into two cottages in the late 17th or early 18th century. Another cottage to the north has been replaced by the butcher's shop. It was granted to Henry and Elizabeth Bowbrook by the Lord of the Manor in 1682. The Frosts owned from 1748 to 1800.

(20) Hawthorn and Vine Cottages, are timber-framed and date from about 1630.  There is much re-used timber, including a notable steeply cambered tie-beam with plain crown post and some smoke-blackened rafters which would seem to have come from an open hall house. The chimney at the north end of Hawthorn Cottage retains a salt box and bacon cupboard. The roof has through clasped side-purlins set in nine-inch notches in the principal rafters, collars and queen struts. The bay on the south side of Vine Cottage is probably an 18th century addition. The front addition to Hawthorn Cottage in polygonal stone is dated 1875. The first manor reference is in 1725 when the cottage is granted to John Borer.

(21) Rose Cottage, formerly the central part of a block of cottages, consisted originally  of two storeys facing east, one room deep with a chimney at the north end. It was built in the first half of the 18th century probably about 1730. The roof has very light rafters, through side-purlins and angle struts. A Victorian addition to the rear provided a second room on each floor. Manor record says that John Stone held in 1732 and from 1732 to 1825 it belonged to the Balchins.

(22) Jasmine Cottage, formerly White House, is timber-framed but with light timbers

and through braces, built just after 1800 on part of Southlands on Hazel Hall estate. Low pitched slate roof with angle struts. At time of the Tithe Map 1843, it was occupied by Thomas Childers who also had a carpenter's shop opposite.

(23) Lawbrook, consisted originally of a small two-storey house built in coursed

random rubble with a small area of garnetting and a chimney in the early to mid 17th century. This is close to the cliff face at the back of the present main house. It had a stone-lined well (now under the modern kitchen) and a cellar excavated from the rock. The main block was added to the south by a wealthy person about 1850-60. The drawing room to the west was lavishly redecorated about 1890. The rear block to the east, with a seven-light window, is high quality Edwardian work. The name Leybrook is found in manor records of 1560 and the will of Arthur Haughton of 1684 leaves to his wife and daughter 'Lands, Tenements and Barns called Lawbrooke, lately purchased of the co-heirs of Collins deceased'. Lawbrook belonged to the Callinghams 1767-1808 and the Woods and their Goldhawk heirs 1808-66. During this time the grand new block may have been built by Arthur Onslow, who is said to have taken it, presumably as a tenant, in 1854. It became part of the Cubitt estate in 1866 and their tenant, T Owen, probably did the 1890 decorations, while the next owners, General and Mrs Smeaton (1910-25), did the Edwardian work.

(24) Oak Farm, formerly Jessie's Farm House, Burges or Customary Lands is of

Bargate stone with brick dressing and string course of three bricks with a course of bricks on either side. It has two storeys, attics and a cellar under the south-east end. The main chimney stack at the north-west end has hooks for bacon smoking. This was the main living room/kitchen with a parlour at the other end. It was probably built early in the 18th century. A new kitchen/scullery added at the back about 1800; oven and fireplace remain. A house seems to have been here in 1635 belonging to Thomas Freland who then sold to John Hillier. In 1643 it was bought by John Bignold, owner of the King John House tannery in Gomshall. In the 18th century, Ameys owned and then Woods from whom it became part of the Hazel Hall estate in the 19th century. The present house may have been built by William Amey.

(25) Lane End Farm, formerly Tillings or Stilleys in a lane called Stillywent, has a house described as modern in 1919. However the very substantial farm buildings contain barns with angle strut roofs of the early 19th century, and brick buildings around yards with a central brick granary and mill house of about 1850-60. Records go back to 1532 when John Weller owned the land, late Thomas Tilling's. In the 18th century the Ameys owned and then the Woods from whom it became part of the Goldhawk's Hazel Hall estate. It was probably farmed by the Goldhawks early in the 19th century as a beam in the barn is inscribed 'RG 1808'. In 1866 it is described as having a small farm house occupied as five labourers' tenements. The mid 19th century farm buildings were erected either by Goldhawks or by the Cubitt estate after 1866.

RAD LANE

WONHAM WAY

HOE

PURSERS LANE

BROADFIELD ROAD

BURROWS CROSS

JESSES LANE

24

LAWBROOK LAN

← TO SHERE **23**

| 0 m | 500 m |

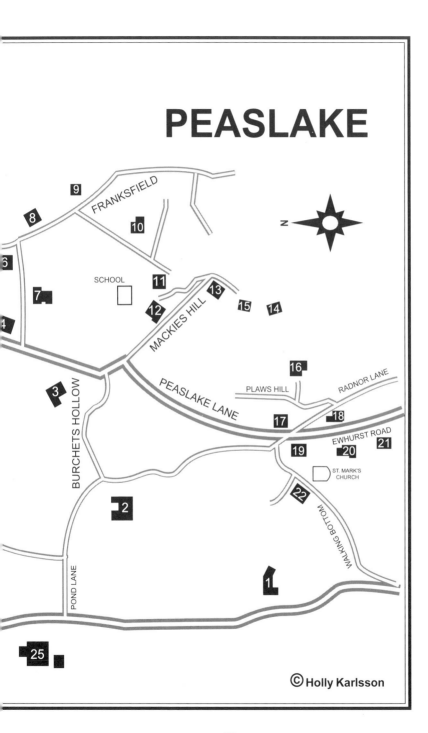

PEASLAKE

OLD HOUSES IN SHERE VILLAGE

UPPER STREET: NORTH SIDE

(1) Gareth and Old Cottage, formerly Burden's in the Manor of Shere Vachery, retains

the solar wing from a house of about 1450, the rest of which was replaced about 1500 by a timber-framed two-bay open hall. Altered to a smoke-bay house between 1540 and 1640 by a Parkhurst or a Risbridger. A chimney was inserted about 1640. Gareth is partly modern, but includes some of the open hall. The garnetted brick front is later 17th century.

(2) Burrowdown, a brick house with nice detailing, built about 1865 by the Duke of

Northumberland (owner of Albury Park). The land was a part of Cottells where there had been two 17th century houses and a blacksmith's.

(3) Anchor Cottage and Pilgrim's Garth, on another part of Cottells, probably land

which was part of the farm called Cottells or belonging to the Cottell family. Possibly on the site of an open hall house. Built about 1600, timber-framed, with two cross-wings; a house of some importance. May at one time have been the Old Anchor public house. Alterations, mostly to its appearance only, made about 1880. Used by J M Barrie in 1892 as a holiday cottage.

(4) Burdens, was part of Burden's in Shere Eborum Manor. Timber-framed, about

1625 at the earliest, much repaired and altered. Built by the Bignold family, who were related to the Poulters who owned for 150 years.

(5A) Western Cottages & (5B) The Manor House Lodge, respectively west and east

of Tudor Cottage, were designed by Edwin Lutyens for Reginald Bray and built in 1894. (Manor House no.55).

(6) Tudor Cottage, formerly Smith's, a three-bay timber-framed open hall house with

internal jetty and smoke-blackened rafters, built in the early 15th century by the Sayer family. A bay was added about the time James Sayer is recorded as owner in 1571. A chimney was inserted about 1620, perhaps by William White. The Hooker family, weavers, owned 1745-83, when it was bought by William Bray in exchange for Rolls (7). A hat (possibly Tudor) discovered in 1972 concealed beside the chimney is on display in the Shere Museum (40A).

(7) Vine Cottages, formerly Rolls, a small farm of some seven acres. Timber-framed,

two-bay open hall house of about 1500, with crown-post roof, built perhaps by William Bound. At the west end, the front part was rebuilt in the early 17th century as an elegant parlour (some panelling survives): behind it, the late 14th century bay, with a crown-post roof, may have been a kitchen, originally detached. The jettied eastern wing, of about 1500, with a crown-post roof, was probably the 'King's Arms' public house some years before the whole was bought by William Bray in 1782 and shortly thereafter exchanged with James Hooker for Smith's (6). A plan of 1724 shows two orchards and a hop-garden.

UPPER STREET: SOUTH SIDE

(8) Waitlands and Knapps Cottage. Apparently that part of Cottells called the Seven

Elms, and originally two separate cottages, each a two-bay, timber-framed chimney house. Knapp's Cottage, with flint infilling, was built about 1660, Waitland's slightly earlier. They were joined together later. The builder may have been Abraham Sands, a Guildford saddler, who also owned two houses across the road (2). His daughter, Bethia Sands, lived here in the early 18th century. William Bray became the owner in 1799.

(9) Denton, formerly the small farm of Knaveshurst. Originally timber-framed, three

bays, and built about 1550, possibly by a Lawrence. The two-bay room at the rear may have had some special, non-domestic purpose.The Kelsey family of yeomen and weavers owned 1620-94, as did Humphrey Denton, also a yeoman and weaver, and then his heirs, about 1700-72. For many years the base of the Norton family's decorating and undertaking business.

(10) Lime Cottage, another part of Knaveshurst, a timber-framed hall house of the

early 16th century (possibly more extensive than now), floored over in the next century. The brick addition (subsequently joined) to the east end was built about 1830 as a detached shop by a Shere grocer, Solomon Sutton.

(11) Denmarke, formerly Clark's, probably a small farm, a four-bay timber-framed

house, with a fine upper room fronting the road, perhaps originally jettied, and possibly the meeting-place for the manorial court (Shere Vachery) (compare 24). Never an open hall house, it might have been a parlour wing at right angles to an earlier, vanished house. A date of about 1560-80 is suggested by the early side-purlin roof. Refaced and converted into cottages around 1725. An original window (beside the chimney and facing west) is visible from the street. The outbuilding beside the road was probably put up before 1700. The property was owned by William Kelsey before 1635 and by successive Kelseys until 1717.

(12) Fernside was originally part of Clark's (11), being converted from a malthouse in

1714 when sold by Francis Kelsey, yeoman of Clark's, to William Jeffery, a barber-surgeon. The west end was for many years the Weller family's off-licence shop.

(13) Bignolds and Beulah Cottage (now linked), part of the neighbouring Hawkin's

(14). The oldest remaining part is the eastern, the present Bignold's, a one-and-a-half storey timber-framed central chimney house of about 1640, with a fine fireplace and spit-rack. Beulah Cottage, also timber-framed, was added a few years later as a two-bay single storey workshop or store-room, extended about 1800 with a bay at the west end. The property was sold in 1674 by the owner of Hawkin's to David Ede of Shere, cooper. Still a cooper's in 1798 when sold by Thomas Crouch to William Bray; let to William Bignold - cooper - after whose family the older part is still named.

(14) Old Manor Cottages, formerly an important house called Hawkin's. Two jettied

cross-wings and part of the centre remain from a timber-framed hall house of about 1500, though it is not certain whether the hall was an open hall. The cross-wings have crown-post roofs; the western wing (now No. 3) was probably the original parlour, and the eastern wing (now No.1) the original service part. The house was probably built by the Sayer family, owners for about a hundred years in the 15th and 16th centuries. The Rev. Richard Smith, Rector of Shere 1612-52, became the owner and seems to have lived here 1630-52. William Bray (1736-1832) bought it in 1766 and lived here from 1773, making substantial alterations, a process continued by his daughter Catherine when it became her home. It was divided up after her death in 1854. The height of the central part has been reduced. (For the bridge, see 55A).

(15 & 15A) June Garden, a timber-framed double pile house built about 1610 on land

previously part of Palfremans (24) and sold off by the Risbridgers, who had just bought the manor of Shere Eborum. This property was acquired in 1772 by Henry Hunt, wheelwright, already the occupier. The Hunt family carried on their wheelwright and gunsmith business here for many years. Richard Hunt appears to have built the neighbouring pair of houses, Little House and June Cottage (15A), on the eastern part of his property, about 1820, possibly for his workmen. After his death in 1854 his three daughters inherited and Miss Hunt lived in June Garden for over fifty years. Considerable alterations were made about 1850.

(16) Elm Cottage, formerly Gibble's, an end chimney two-bay timber-framed house

with a stair turret, built probably about 1620, belonged to the Kelsey family for most of the 17th century and then to the Bignolds. It was bought by William Bray in 1771. The Harris family, millers, lived here for part of the 19th century. The back room may have been a weaver's premises. A pot-quern of medieval type, discovered during alterations here in the rubble underneath an old bread-oven, is discussed in the 1964 volume of the "Surrey Archaeological Collections".

(17) Manor Cottage, formerly Shares, was built in the late 15th century, possibly a

weaver's house, timber-framed in four narrow bays, and with a crown-post roof. The two central bays were probably an open hall. The earliest documentation of a house here is from 1503, when it belonged to George Parkhurst. Bought by William Bray in 1772. In the 1920's, it included the Misses Batcock's sweet shop.

GOMSHALL LANE

(18) Former and present Village Halls, built on land once part of Rolls Farm (7) and

thence part of the Netley estate in the 19th century. The brick hall was built in 1897 (Queen Victoria's Diamond Jubilee) and the pebbledashed hall in 1920 to commemorate the 1914-18 war. The earlier hall subsequently housed the Shere Working Men's Club (now defunct).

(19) Seaforth Cottage, formerly Hangman's Croft in Shere Eborum manor. Timber-

framed, built in 1632 by William Blackman on land part of a farm called Cossons (see 47). Considerably altered about 1860 by Sir Henry Cole (first director of the V.& A.) renting from the Frasers of Netley. One of his guests was W M Thackeray, who wrote part of his novel "The Virginians" here. Later occupied by the Read family, who added the butcher's shop. Ernest Read, conductor and founder of the Children's Orchestra and Concerts, was born here in 1879.

(20) Kinghams Restaurant, formerly Oak Cottage and before that Hangman's in

Shere Vachery manor, a one-and-a-half storey timber-framed house built seemingly with an end chimney which became a central chimney when a bay was added to the western end in the 1640's. The builder was William Blackman, owner of the adjoining Hangman's Croft (19), and the land (acquired by him) had previously been part of a farm called Catherine's (41). Included in the Netley estate in the 19th century. There are late 17th and 18th century additions; the rear wing is modern.

(21) The Queen's Mead, two acres, between Gomshall Lane, the Tillingbourne and the back of the properties in Middle Street, has been built on only in comparatively recent times (telephone exchanges, business units, Weller's Court, etc.). It was leased in 1550 by Sir Edward Bray to John Parkhurst of Speers (25). It went with Speers until 1811 and then with Sayers (31).

(22, 22A & 22B) High House Meadow to the east has provided the sites for the School buildings (22A), erected in 1842, about 1856, and about 1870 (see the plaques on them), and for the Shere Swimming Pool (22B), created in 1891, the gift of Lady Arthur Russell, and reputed to be the oldest outdoor public swimming-pool in the country.

MIDDLE STREET

(23) The Old Wall and the Well. The wall runs from Elm Cottage (16) to Manor Cottage

(17), then continues curving round to Forge Cottage (24). Built by William Bray in 1772, when he also pulled down a decayed cottage (another part of Palfreman's) which had stood between Elm and Manor Cottages. The well was dug in 1886, 286 feet deep, through running sand, and was presented to the village by the two Misses Spottiswoode of Drydown on the Ewhurst road.

(24) Forge Cottage and Bodryn, formerly Palfreman's. Forge Cottage is the hall and

service wing, with crown-post roof, surviving from a timber-framed open hall house built perhaps as early as the 14th century. Bodryn, the timber-framed two-bay cross-wing with a clasped-purlin roof and jettied front, is a 16th century rebuild in grander style of the parlour end. An early owner was Oliver Sands (died 1512), to whom there is a memorial in Shere parish church. Next the Risbridger family owned until 1610 in which year there was a grant to hold a manor court here. According to John Hassell's watercolour it was still known as the "Court House" in 1823, the manor concerned being Shere Eborum (compare 11). For well over a century owned by the Bound family and their heirs until bought in 1771 by William Bray, who lived here for a year or two, when it was described as "the Little House", before he moved into "the Great House" of Hawkin's (14). The Bristows' butcher's shop appears to have been here in the early 19th century, and later it was Puttock and Baverstock, blacksmiths.

(25) Row of shops, formerly Speers, whose land originally extended south to the

manorial waste beside the Tillingbourne. A fine timber-framed merchant's open hall house of the later 15th century, of which only the southern cross-wing with its crown-post roof survives. The original central open hall was replaced, incorporating a chimney and continuous front jetty, about 1600, for the Parkhursts. The northern four-bay cross-wing, with its good panelling, was built, replacing the original parlour end, early in the 17th century, almost certainly by John Stonell, a fustian weaver, who bought Speers in 1603 from the Parkhursts' heirs and whose looms may have been on the ground floor at this end. By about 1760 this had become a shop (Buchanan's grocery in the late 18th century), as it has been ever since. Bank Terrace (25A) in Gomshall Lane is a 19th century conversion of outbuildings, while at the north-east corner of Speers the 17th century Woodbine Cottage has been incorporated (after alterations) into Lloyds TSB Bank (25B).

(26 & 26A) The east side of Middle Street formerly contained the tenement called

Rogers', once a part of Speers but later a separate property. A large barn here is mentioned as early as 1576, and in the first half of the 19th century Thomas Mills' fellmonger's business used it but it was pulled down shortly afterwards. The present Chantry House (formerly Durfold, 26A) was built in 1867 and the other buildings are later Victorian.

(27, 27A, 27B & 27C) The west side of Middle Street has, on the site of a barn erected

in 1659, a timber-built blacksmith's forge (27A) which was refronted in 1914 with old timbers reputedly from the Rogers' barn opposite. The shop (currently a restaurant - 27B) was designed for the Bray estate about 1892 by the young Edwin Lutyens in a style to harmonise with the older buildings. Further south, towards the stream, is the Shere and Albury Volunteer Fire Brigade station, dated 1885, and converted to public toilets in 1977 (27C).

(28 & 28A) The Pound, next to the Tillingbourne, appears to have been moved to this

site in the mid-19th century from a similar position on the east side of the street, but an earlier pound was at the western end of Upper Street, the field where Coombe End (53) now stands being recorded in 1701 as Shere's Pound Field. The Bridge (28A) over the stream dates from the 18th century.

AROUND THE SQUARE

(29 & 29A) High House, formerly called 'the farm house of Shere', was the principal house in the Manor of Shere Eborum. It is recorded as a capital mansion house in 1577 when it was sold by Lady Jane Bray, third wife of the first Sir Edward Bray, to Catherine and William Risbridger who already held a lease. This early house, however, must have been pulled down by the Risbridgers, as the present house was built about 1630-40, probably by William Risbridger, grandson of the purchaser. This is a brick house, the courses in English bond, with a queen-strut roof, of two storeys plus attics, having two rooms on each floor and a central chimney. There are spit-machine marks on the fireplace in the easternmost downstairs room, which would have been the kitchen, the other ground-floor room being the parlour. Additions were made in Victorian times. The nearby farm buildings (29A) include a timber-framed granary (17th or 18th century) and two barns, one of about 1880 and the other dated 1786, when it was put up by William Bray who had bought back the manor, farmhouse and farm in 1771 from Thomas Page. The earliest documentary reference to the name 'High House' is on the 1772 Bray estate map.

(30) The former Petts stood on a site now part of the front garden of Sayers (31). Sometime before 1600 it was the 'George' alehouse and, according to tradition, a hostel for pilgrims. It might in the late 15th and early 16th centuries have been the Church House, acting as a community centre and hosting the church ales, festivities which raised revenue for the church. Like the other buildings on the north side of the Square, it may have originally been an encroachment onto the market-place.

(31) Sayers (known as Burnside in the 19th century and until 1942), brick-built to an L-shape in 1797 by Thomas Weatherhead, master cooper of Wapping, who married Mary Buchanan of Shere, whose father owned the 'White Horse' (38). It is on the site of a 1610 tenement called The Queen's Pound. Owned by the Cave family 1811-70 and then by the the Davey, Poulter and Forrest families, the latter being the proprietors of the once widespread Forrest's Stores chain of shops. Rented 1895-1959 by the Hyde family. William Hyde was a landscape painter and book illustrator, and a close friend of Hilaire Belloc, providing the pictures for his "The Old Road" (the putative Pilgrims' Way) and for volumes of "The Victoria County Histories" as well as for publications by George Meredith, Shelley, Milton and Alice Meynell.

(32) Pantrys and Minns Cottage (5, The Square). The east end is an early 17th century two-storey stone house, with 18th century brick front, attics and butt-purlin roof. There is a very good, though late, spit-rack for the chimney inglenook which was once thought to have been the kitchen of Petts (30). Owned by the Lipscombe family in the 18th century; by William Southon, shopkeeper and owner of Gomshall Mill, prior to 1850; and by William Harding 1854-79.

(33) Old Way and Grove Cottages appear to have been the property called in the  manor records 'a house in Shere Street near the church'. It was originally one house, timber-framed, of one-and-a-half storeys, with Grove Cottage a cross-wing to Old Way Cottage. A through-side-purlin roof with queen-struts, but difficult to date; it is probably the early 17th century cottage belonging then to the Goddards. William Southon was the owner about 1840.

(34) A Barn in Shere Street stood south of the stream, built in the mid-16th century and owned in the 18th by the Duncumb family (Rectors of Shere). It was purchased in 1853 by William Harding, pulled down after 1861, and a pair of brick cottages were built on the site some decades later.

(35 & 35A) Rookery Nook, the Shop and part of Haven Cottage formed the original Gallants, on a site of some importance

(conjecturally the early manorial centre) occupying the whole south side of the Square. Built about 1450-1500, it was probably a single-storey open hall house, its parlour end (with garderobe) to the east and its service end to the west. In the late 16th century this fine Wealden-style house was rebuilt as a continuous jetty by inserting a central section. Owned by the Redford family for most of the 16th century and then by John Goddard who also owned property on the north side of the Square (33). By 1700 it included a blacksmith's on the site of the present shop. The Nye, Bignold, Longhurst and Jelley families were blacksmith owners until 1878 when the smithy was converted into a grocery shop for George Sanders and his wife, formerly Ann Jelley. There was a partial rebuild of the shop after a fire in 1890. The Cottage and the other part of Haven Cottage (35A) are late 18th /early 19th century additions.

(36) Vaughans was a separate part of Gallants with, originally, a passageway to its  east. It has a side-purlin, queen-strut roof, is of two bays, and was built about 1550, probably by the Redfords, with some rebuilding in the late 17th century. John Nye's will (1718) instructed Thomas Bignold to sell off this part of Gallant's to his tailor friend Edward Ventrice. It changed hands several times, becoming William Southon's 1813-50; it was probably during this latter period that it became a baker's shop. Afterwards it belonged to the Jelley family, then to the Sanders family. For most of that time it was occupied by the Vaughans (bakers) after whom it was named. The village post office was here from before 1871 to 1894.

(37) Gallandes, another part of Gallants, seems to have been built about 1742 - the date on one of its bricks. In 1773 it was sold by Thomas Bignold to William Frost, schoolmaster, already the occupier. The Frost family owned throughout the 19th century.

(38) The White Horse, formerly a house called Cripps, was originally a two-bay timber-framed open hall house of about 1450, with twin service rooms to the north and two-bay cross-wings at both parlour and service ends. About 1600 a chimney with fine stone back-to-back fireplaces was inserted in the parlour end of the hall, and the hall reframed with a continuous jetty. The external timbering was applied about 1920. References date back to 1562. In 1624 it belonged to Richard Francis, and this family, prominent in Shere in the 16th century, may have owned at that earlier period. It belonged, 1664-1730, to inn-holders called Sherlock, becoming an inn in the late 17th century, when the roof was rebuilt, there was a refronting in brick, and a cellar and detached brewhouse were added. Various owners included the Buchanans in the first half of the 19th century (31), and the inn was managed by the Askew family, 1866-1945, when it was a haunt of literary and artistic figures.

(39) Lavender House, formerly part of Cripps (38), was converted, apparently in the mid 19th century, from outbuildings, and included a butcher's shop and then tea-rooms before becoming a residence.

SHERE LANE

(40 & 40A) South of The White Horse, the adjoining land (on the west side of Shere

Lane) was known as Marysse. It included a hop garden. The 'Prince of Wales', formerly Cook's Beer House, was built on part of this land in the late 18th. century, the Classical frontage being an early 20th century addition. Further south is the Malthouse (40A), built about 1830, which supplied Reffells, the owners of the 'Black Horse' at Gomshall. The Malthouse is now the home of the Shere Museum.

(41) Dial Cottage (formerly Juden), a part of Catherine's (see 20), is a three-bay, two-

storey timber-framed house with a side-purlin and queen-strut roof, and an integral central chimney; though the date '1622' is inscribed on the stack, it could be slightly later. A face-wing was added about 1675 and there are modern additions. The house belonged to Thomas Hill in the 17th century, and was bought by William Bray in 1771.

(42) Knaveshurst, a brick and Bargate stone two-bay end-chimney house of the late

17th century, enlarged in the 18th. In the early 19th century, a large 'industrial' addition was constructed against the street front, probably by the Bristow family, owning and using the premises as a butcher's with a slaughterhouse in the grounds.

(43) Yew Trees and Trenchmore. Most of the older structure is in Yew Trees. The

original early 17th century timber-framed house was of one-and-a-half storeys and two bays with an end chimney. A third bay (now part of Trenchmore) was added on the north, perhaps as a parlour. The roof is of queen-strut and clasped-purlin construction. The name Trenchmore is old (e.g., as a local surname about 1200), and Shere Eborum manor records indicate a house on Trenchmore's land in 1609 when it was owned by Richard Lawrence, who may have built the house. He also owned Knaveshurst in Upper Street (9,10). In the mid 18th century William Wickham was the owner and in 1792 it was acquired by John Groom, surgeon; his son Henry, also a doctor, lived here after him. Extensive additions were made about 1860 and 1880.

LOWER STREET

(44) Nos. 1-4, Lower Street, parts of the former Stiles. No.1 appears in the records

about 1700. Originally a one-room single-storey stone building, it was enlarged to a two-storey house with a brick front and side-purlin roof about 1705, probably by John and Dorothy Wild. Their initials and that date appear over the former entrance. Thomas Frost owned it (as well as 45, to the west) and later in the 19th century it was John Sherman's butcher's shop. No. 2 represents the parlour wing, end-on to the road, of a medieval house extending to the west but now replaced by Victorian rebuilding.

(45) Willow and Ash Cottages, formerly a part of Stiles. Built about 1475 as a single-

bay hall recessed in Wealden fashion with a two-storey, one-bay wing at each end and a crown-post roof. About 1550 a floor and a chimney were inserted into the hall, the chimney having a fine wooden surround and a splendid spit-rack, probably Jacobean. There are notable hollow mouldings on the jetty fascia boards. Johanna Sands, wife of Oliver Sands of Palfreman's (24), owned in 1524, having inherited, possibly from Henry Styles. A manor court roll of 1563 refers to a grant of a house and two acres made before 1300 by the then lord of the manor to William the Carpenter, who may have been the father of Christine Carpenter, the anchoress of Shere, who was enclosed in her cell at the Church in 1329. For most of the 16th century this property belonged to the Risbridgers, and in the 18th century to the Harding family. It was at some time the 'White Hart' public house, according to a court roll of 1839. Thomas Frost, saddler, was the owner in the early 19th century, but from 1822 it appears to have been John Hersee's wheelwright's, remaining a wheelwright's for the rest of the 19th century.

(46) The Old Forge, formerly Smith's, is a small two-bay timber-framed house with a

queen-strut roof, much altered, but probably built in the first half of the 17th century by Henry White. When William Bray purchased it in 1795 it included Edward Lambert's butcher's shop, and in the 19th century it became part of John Hersee's wheelwright's, with a forge in the outshot.

(47) The Old Prison was formerly part of a substantial holding called Cossons (19),  the main buildings of which stood between Lower Street and the stream but were demolished about 1786. The Old Prison is a small timber-framed two-storey house, with a through-purlin and queen-strut roof, built probably in the early 17th century, with then a smoke bay and one room on either side on each floor. The smoke bay was removed and a chimney added about 1650. The front wing, said to have been used as the local lock-up, may have been added at the same time: it retains its barred window. The house was probably built by Oliver White, whose daughter Ann married the first John Harding and inherited in 1652. The Harding family owned for a hundred years. Bought by William Bray in 1761. Mrs. Emma Diggins, the Church caretaker, kept a sweetshop here about 1900.

(48) Weavers House, a part of Hampshire's, is a 19th century successor to an earlier  house on the site, and was probably built by John Tanner, the owner 1783-1839.

(49) Wickhams and Weyside, a two-storey timber-framed house, was probably built  about 1650. It has a side-purlin, queen-strut roof. There is a notable smoke bay which was later used as a bacon loft. Manor Court roll entries begin in 1636. William White, the owner of Tudor Cottage (6), bought it in 1646 and may have rebuilt this house before selling Tudor Cottage in 1648. John Wickham bought it in 1727 and dying aged 90 in 1771 left it to his daughter Elizabeth Tanner. By 1822 the house was in decay but was repaired by Thomas Randall.

RECTORY LANE AND THE NORTH-WEST OUTSKIRTS

(50) The Old Rectory was built in 1844 and enlarged in 1859; it ceased to be the  rectory in 1950. The architects were Garland and Christopher, of the Adelphi, London, and it was built to replace an old timber-framed parsonage-house which formerly stood on lower ground nearer the Tillingbourne and which had fallen into decay. This older house (shown in a painting by Hassell and mentioned by John Aubrey in his county history of Surrey) had been surrounded by a moat. In his 'Diary', John Evelyn records dining here in 1677 with one of the Duncumb family who were the successive Rectors of Shere 1658-1843.

(51) Workshop Cottage is a small timber-framed house of two bays and one-and-a-

half storeys with a side-purlin roof. It was probably built by a poor owner about 1680-1720, on part of a field originally belonging to Burdens in Upper Street (4) and owned by the Beldam family. It seems to have been part of the property bought by Thomas Miall in 1737, continuing in Miall ownership until 1829 when it was bought by the Misses Malthus of Albury who had previously purchased The Cottage (52) from Thomas Miall. The poet William Allingham and his wife Helen, the artist, stayed in this house in 1878, when she painted some of her earliest cottage scenes.

(52) Pound House and The Cottage appear to have been originally a very small three-

storey house built into the hillside sometime between 1625 and 1725 and later given a Georgian front, probably during the first half of the 18th century by either John Beldam, a maltster of Shere, or Thomas Miall, carpenter, the owners during that period. It seems that it was used by the Miall family as a house and carpenter's shop until bought in 1807 by the Misses Malthus and enlarged by them. It was then left to their sister Mary Ann Catherine Bray (the widow of Edward Bray) who lived here 1837-52.

(53) Coombe End was built in 1838 for Augustus Warren, attorney, who had married

Harriet Bray in 1818. The site was once a bean-field belonging to the Albury estate but in 1701 was recorded as Shere's Pound Field, the Pound being situated at that time near the present junction of Upper Street and Rectory Lane. (See 28 for the present Pound).

(54) The Lodge was built about 1802 by William Bray for his son Edward. The land

seems to have included Allen's Cottage, built before 1654 and used during the 18th century as a parish house for the poor. When William Bray acquired the land in 1802 he gave as a replacement parish house a cottage in Rectory Lane, apparently on the site now occupied by April Cottage (54A), while Allen's Cottage (now vanished) may have become the outbuildings shown on the Tithe Map of 1843, opposite the junction with Rectory Lane. Edward Bray occupied Shere Lodge (as it was then called) until 1814, followed by his son Edward 1837-66. At other times it was let. Substantial alterations were made in 1869 and part of the older portion was taken down about 1925.

(55 & 55A) The Manor House originally called Firhill, was built for Reginald Bray in a neo-

Tudor style about 1844 on part of the demesne lands of the Manor of Shere Eborum. It was enlarged in the 1880s for Sir Reginald More Bray and renamed the Manor House in 1888. William Bray's former garden at Hawkin's (14) became the kitchen garden of the Manor House and was connected to the Manor grounds by a footbridge over Upper Street; the present bridge (55A) dates from 1911.

EWHURST ROAD (WEST SIDE), SOUTH OF SHERE VILLAGE

(56) Cotterells House, formerly West Cottells, consists of a 17th century farmhouse of two builds at the back and an early 18th century block at the front, facing the road. Both have roofs with butt-side-purlins, not in line, the front blocks being of lighter construction. An earlier house here had been bought from Thomas, grandson of Oliver Sands (died in 1512) in the mid 16th century by the Risbridger family and the 1680-period work was probably for John Risbridger. The Risbridgers sold in 1700 to John Sherlock of Bramley, and the new front block may have been built then. The Sherlock family continuing to own, John's great-grandaughter Catherine (wife of John Hicks) inherited in 1794; their son sold in 1815 to Richard Sparkes, whose family owned until 1864. The smaller farm opposite, now Little Cotterells, was known as East Cottells and is documented back to the 1620s.

(57) Hound House, formerly Greet's or Gritt's, was owned by the Parkhurst family from about 1500 to 1813. A three-bay medieval hall house was extended, probably by Robert Parkhurst about 1580, by adding three bays to the north with a clasped-purlin and queen-strut roof. Chimneys were added later. Adjoining this is a block converted about 1800 from farm buildings to cottages, with a nice bread-oven and a well in the angle between it and the old farmhouse. In 1813 Catherine, wife of John Sherlock of Bramley, and her son William, sold to John Sparkes who in 1815 built the Regency villa style front part of the house with its Greek Doric porch facing the road. A large block was added to the north before 1850. The farm buildings include a late 17th century timber-framed and brick-infilled granary, and two old barns, one of around 1700 (consisting of two buildings moved and joined) and one (also moved) from the 18th century. The fine stable block is part of the early 19th century 'planned' farmyard. Legend says that King John had a hunting lodge here where he kept his hounds. Records show that the Rev. Samuel Godshall, who lived at Albury, kept hounds here towards the end of the 18th century. He founded the Union (now Surrey Union) Hunt. The name 'Hound House' instead of Greet's first appears in a manor record of 1781.

INDEX OF SHERE HOUSES

No. on plan **Present name of House**

1. Gareth and Old Cottage
2. Burrowdown
3. Anchor Cottage and Pilgrim's Garth
4. Burdens
5A Western Cottages
5B The Manor House Lodge
6. Tudor Cottage
7. Vine Cottages
8. Waitlands and Knapps Cottage
9. Denton
10. Lime Cottage
11. Denmarke
12. Fernside
13. Bignolds and Beulah Cottage
14. Old Manor Cottages
15. June Garden
15A Little House and June Cottage
16. Elm Cottage
17. Manor Cottage
18. Former and present Village Halls
19. Seaforth Cottage
20. Kinghams Restaurant
21. The Queen's Mead
22. High House meadow
22A School
22B Swimming Pool
23. The Old Wall and The Well
24. Forge Cottage and Bodryn
25. Row of Shops
25A Bank Terrace
25B Lloyds TSB Bank formerly Woodbine Cottage
26. The East Side of Middle Street
26A Chantry House
27. The West Side of Middle Street
27A Blacksmith's Forge
27B The Shop

No. on plan **Present name of House**

27C Old Fire Station
28. The Pound
28A The Tillingbourne Bridge
29 High House
29A The Old Farm
30. The former Petts
31. Sayers
32. Pantrys & Minns Cottage
33. Old Way and Grove Cottages
34. A barn in Shere Street
35. Rookery Nook
35A Haven Cottage and The Cottage
36. Vaughans
37. Gallandes
38. The White Horse
39. Lavender House
40. South of The White Horse
40A Shere Museum -The Malthouse
41. Dial Cottage
42. Knaveshurst
43. Yew Trees and Trenchmore
44. Nos.1-4, Lower Street
45. Willow and Ash Cottages
46. The Old Forge
47. The Old Prison
48. Weavers House
49. Wickhams and Weyside
50. The Old Rectory
51. Workshop Cottage
52. Pound House and The Cottage
53. Coombe End
54. The Lodge
54A April Cottage
55. The Manor House
55A Footbridge (private)
56. Cottrells House
57. Hound House